D1172734

Yellow Umbrella Books are published by Capstone Press
151 Good Counsel Drive, P.O. Box 669, Mankato, Minnesota 56002
www.capstonepress.com

Library of Congress Cataloging-in-Publication Data
VanVoorst, Jennifer, 1972–
    Working / by Jennifer VanVoorst.
    p. cm.
    Summary: Simple text and photographs present a variety of familiar occupations.
    ISBN 0-7368-2910-5 (hardcover)—ISBN 0-7368-2869-9 (softcover)
    1. Occupations—Juvenile literature. 2. Work—Juvenile literature. [1. Occupations.
2. Work.] I. Title.
HF5381.2.V367 2004
331.7—dc21   2003009323

Editorial Credits
Editorial Director: Mary Lindeen
Editor: Jennifer VanVoorst
Photo Researcher: Wanda Winch
Developer: Raindrop Publishing

Photo Credits
Cover: Keith Brofsky/PhotoDisc; Title Page: Michael Ventura/Folio, Inc.; Page 2:
John A. Rizzo/PhotoDisc; Page 3: Bruce Ando/Image Ideas, Inc.; Page 4: C. Borland/
PhotoLink/PhotoDisc; Page 5: Creatas; Page 6: Jim Foell/Capstone Press; Page 7:
Royalty-Free/Corbis; Page 8: HIRB/Index Stock Imagery; Page 9: Geostock/
PhotoDisc; Page 10: StockTrek/PhotoDisc; Page 11: Mark Andersen/RubberBall
Productions; Page 12: Richard T. Nowitz/Folio, Inc.; Page 13: Comstock; Page 14:
Royalty-Free/Corbis; Page 15: Keith Brofsky/PhotoDisc; Page 16: SW Productions/
PhotoDisc

1 2 3 4 5 6 09 08 07 06 05 04

Working

by Jennifer VanVoorst

Consultant: Dwight Herold, EdD, Past President,
Iowa Council for the Social Studies

Yellow Umbrella Books

an imprint of Capstone Press
Mankato, Minnesota

You go to school in the morning.
Other people go to work.

People do many different kinds of work.

This man works as a sales person. He helps us buy things.

This woman works as a nurse.
She takes care of us when we
are sick.

This man works as a garbage collector. He keeps our streets clean.

This man works as a farmer.
He grows food for us to eat.

This woman works as a police
officer. She helps keep us safe.

This man works as a teacher.
He helps us learn.

This woman works as an
astronaut. She explores space.

This man works as a carpenter.
He builds things out of wood.

This woman works as a zoo keeper. She takes care of animals at the zoo.

This man works as a truck driver. He moves things from place to place.

This man works as a cook.
He makes food for people to eat.

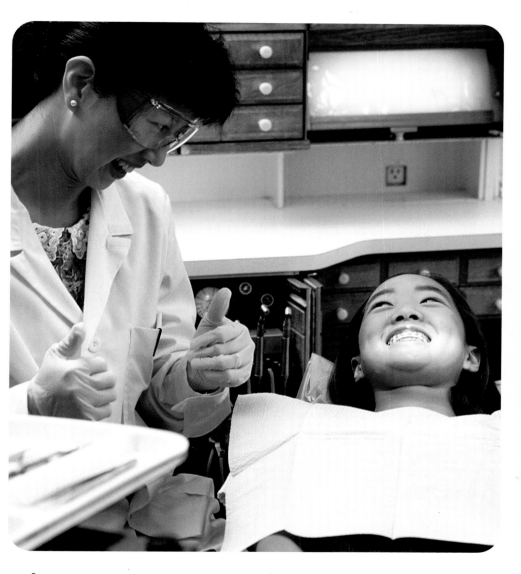

This woman works as a dentist.
She helps us care for our teeth.

What work do you do?

Words to Know/Index

Word Count: 174
Early-Intervention Level: 10

CRANBURY PUBLIC LIBRARY
23 North Main Street
Cranbury, NJ 08512
609-655-0555